BATTLEFIELDS ACROSS AMERICA

SARATOGA

DAVID C. KING

Twenty-First Century Books

Brookfield, Connecticut

Twenty-First Century Books
A Division of The Millbrook Press
2 Old New Milford Road
Brookfield, CT 06804

©1998 by Blackbirch Graphics, Inc.
First Edition
5 4 3 2 1

Printed in the United States of America on acid free paper ∞.

Created and produced in association with Blackbirch Graphics, Inc.

Photo Credits
Pages 4, 6, 7, 9, 10, 12, 16, 20, 22, 24, 27, 28 (top and bottom), 29, 30, 34, 35, 36, 41, 43, 46, 48: North Wind Pictures; pages 50, 52, 56: courtesy of New York State Department of Economic Development; page 55: courtesy of Fort Stanwix National Monument.

All maps by Bob Italiano/© Blackbirch Press, Inc.

Library of Congress Cataloging-in-Publication Data

King, David C.
   Saratoga / David C. King.
      p.   cm. — (Battlefields across America)
   Includes bibliographical references and index.
   Summary: Focuses on the Saratoga battle that would be the turning point of the American Revolution, describes it in the context of the entire war, and examines related sites that can be visited today.
   ISBN 0-7613-3011-9 (lib bdg. : alk. paper)
   1. Saratoga Campaign, 1777—Juvenile literature. [1. Saratoga Campaign, 1777 2. United States—History—Revolution, 1775–1783—Campaigns.] I. Title. II. Series.
E241.S2K56   1998
973.3'33—dc21   97-51204
                                                          CIP
                                                            AC

CONTENTS

THE AMERICAN REVOLUTION:
THE PATRIOTS FIGHT FOR FREEDOM

In the spring of 1775, the people of the 13 British colonies in America went to war against Great Britain. The colonists felt they had to take up arms to defend their rights against an overbearing, tyrannical government. The British viewed the early stages of the Revolution as a foolish rebellion started by a small number of colonists who called themselves "patriots."

The colonies had enjoyed extraordinary prosperity under British rule for more than 150 years. Through their elected assemblies, the colonists could govern their own affairs, pass tax laws, and, for defense, raise volunteer fighting forces called "militias." In the middle of the eighteenth century, however, the British felt the colonists needed to be reminded that the colonies were established for the benefit of Great Britain—the "mother country"—and were expected to obey British laws.

A War for Independence

The trouble between the 13 colonies and Great Britain began after the British, with colonial help, won a long, hard war with France (1756–1763). The British government of King George III and Parliament (the law-making body) decided the colonies should help pay the huge costs of defending and governing the enlarged British Empire. Parliament imposed a series of taxes in the colonies to raise needed funds, but each new tax measure touched off a storm of protest in the colonies.

Between 1763 and 1775, the dispute grew steadily worse. The British insisted on their right to control the colonies in all matters. Many colonists agreed, but a determined minority—the patriots—were equally insistent that only their colonial assemblies had the authority to tax them. In 1773, when some patriots dumped British tea leaves into Boston Harbor to protest a new tea tax, King George III and Parliament decided to take action. They ordered the port of Boston closed and sent a military governor to take control of the colony of Massachusetts. Almost

< 5 >

George III, King of England

a year later, in September 1774, the colonies organized the First Continental Congress. The 56 delegates expressed their displeasure with Great Britain's harsh actions.

The delegates were not demanding independence. They wanted King George to respect the colonists' rights as British citizens. The king and Parliament would not back down from their position, however, or withdraw British troops from Boston. On April 19, 1775, British troops marched inland from Boston to seize patriot weapons. They were met by grim bands of militia at the towns of Lexington and Concord. The fighting that erupted that day marked the beginning of the American Revolution.

To the British, the fighting in Massachusetts was an uprising of a small number of radical patriots. The British did not realize that the patriots, while in the minority, constituted a sizable portion of the population. At the battle of Bunker Hill in June 1775, the Massachusetts militia proved that they would fight, and that they could stand up to the disciplined, battle-hardened British redcoats.

That same month, delegates from the 13 colonies, meeting in Philadelphia as the Second Continental Congress, voted to form some of the militia units into the Continental Army. They named George Washington, of Virginia, commander-in-chief. A year later, in July 1776, the Congress took another bold step when it issued the Declaration of Independence. This eloquent document spelled

< 7 >

out the colonists' grievances against the king and Parliament, severed all ties with Great Britain, and declared that the colonies were now 13 free and independent states. The Americans were fighting for their right to establish a new, independent nation with a government of their own choosing.

Members of the Continental Congress sign the Declaration of Independence.

< 8 >

The British Plan a Traditional War

King George III and most members of Parliament had no intention of giving in to the "rebels." They decided to wage a traditional war against the patriots, fighting in the way that wars were usually fought in Europe. A large army, supported by a fleet of warships, would confront the patriots, defeat them, and the rebellion would be crushed. The king and his ministers in Parliament expected victory within a year.

The Americans, however, did not plan to fight a completely conventional war. General Washington knew that his hastily assembled Continental Army was no match for the larger and more experienced British army. Whenever possible, he avoided the kind of full-scale battle the British counted on.

In Europe, when two armies confronted each other on the battlefield, the people in the villages and countryside stayed out of the way. In America, in addition to Washington's "Continentals," the people of the villages and countryside *were* the army. Wherever the British went, they were swarmed by the local militia, men who fought from the cover of woods and buildings, rather than in the orderly rows of European armies. As soon as a skirmish, or minor fight, was over, the militia seemed to melt away into the forests. As one British officer lamented, "the Americans are nowhere and they are everywhere!"[1]

In June 1775, after the battles of Lexington and Concord and of Bunker Hill, the British in Boston found themselves trapped on the coast by 16,000 American militiamen. Then Washington arrived and began forming the Continental Army by enlisting many of these men. Nine months later, in March 1776, the British decided to evacuate Boston. The British commander, General William Howe, loaded his troops on 125 ships and set sail for the safety of British Canada.

The battles of Lexington and Concord signaled the beginning of the American Revolution.

Encouraged by their success, the patriots were confident that independence would be won within a year. Few were willing to heed the warning of John Adams, who wrote a month after the British evacuation, "We shall have a long, obstinate and bloody war to go through."[2] Adams was right. The war that both sides thought would end in quick victory was to drag on for six long years of uncertainty and hardship.

The Opposing Sides

Great Britain's strongest assets were the world's largest army and a navy that ruled the seas. But these powerful fighting forces were operating far from home. All of the army's weapons and supplies, including much of the food, had to be shipped across the Atlantic. When the redcoats marched inland from the coast, they had to transport all of their supplies overland.

The British faced opposition at home as well as in America. Many Englishmen were unwilling to fight in what they considered to be a

German soldiers (wearing tall helmets) were paid to fight alongside the British.

civil war against fellow British subjects. To raise enough troops, King George III was forced to use German mercenaries—soldiers for hire. Most were from the region of Hesse-Cassel, and these men were called Hessians. Nearly 30,000 Germans fought in the Revolution.

The Patriots

Like the British, the patriots faced strong opposition to their cause on the home front. An estimated 20 percent of the population remained loyal to King George III and Parliament, and about 60,000 of these loyalists fought on the British side. In addition, a number of American Indian tribes agreed to fight for the British, hoping the

< 11 >

British would help them save their tribal lands from land-hungry American settlers. Among these tribes were the powerful Iroquois in New York.

Throughout the war, the Americans had trouble raising and equipping troops. The militia units fought well for short periods, especially when they were close to home. But most militiamen signed up for only a few months of military service. When their time was up, they usually went home rather than sign up for more service. As a result, Washington found it difficult to persuade men to join the Continental Army for the three-year enlistments he felt were necessary. He often found that large segments of his army disappeared when a battle was over. Although a core of determined troops stayed with him throughout the war, he was never able to field an army of more than 20,000 men.

Washington also had to spend much of his time trying to get food, uniforms, and weapons for the Continentals. The Continental Congress was not a national government and had no power to raise money through taxes. Members of the Congress could ask the 13 states to contribute what was needed, but the government of each state tended to assume that the other states should do more.

Despite these problems, the Americans had important strengths, including Washington himself. Even in the most troubled times, he inspired the respect and confidence of his soldiers and of the people. Although Washington experienced more defeats than victories, he always managed to keep the Continental Army in the field, and he wisely avoided risking that army in a full-scale battle.

Perhaps the greatest advantage the Americans had was the strong beliefs of those who supported the patriots' cause. Although less than half the population actively supported the war, those who did were people who were determined to see it through. They were fighting on their own soil, for their freedom and their homes.

George Washington, commander of the Continental Army, won the respect of both soldiers and citizens.

< 13 >

"The Times That Try Men's Souls"

The period from mid-1776 to the autumn of 1777 was a time of great peril for the American cause. Soon after evacuating Boston, the British under Howe struck at Long Island and New York City. In a series of battles at Long Island, Kip's Bay, Harlem Heights, White Plains, and Fort Washington, the British nearly destroyed Washington's Continental Army and took control of New York City.

After several more defeats, Washington retreated with the remnants of his army across New Jersey and into Pennsylvania, with Howe in pursuit. During this dark hour, a young patriot named Thomas Paine wrote a paper called *The Crisis*, which began with these ringing phrases:

> *These are the times that try men's souls. The Summer soldier and the sunshine Patriot will, in this crisis, shrink from the service of their country; but he that stands it now, deserves the love and thanks of man and woman.*[3]

Washington found *The Crisis* so inspiring that he had it read to his men. He also took action. In a daring move, he led his army across the ice-choked Delaware River into New Jersey and won victories at Trenton and Princeton. The stunned British withdrew to New York City, while Washington led his exhausted men into winter quarters in Morristown, New Jersey, where they remained until the spring of 1777.

The British Plan for 1777

In London early in 1777, British Lieutenant General John Burgoyne convinced the government to follow a plan he had developed for ending the war. Burgoyne suggested a three-pronged attack that

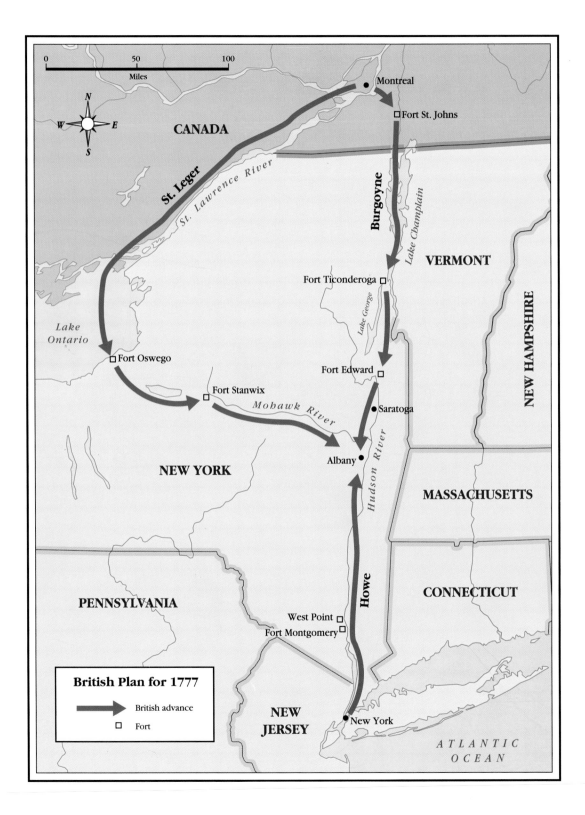

British Plan for 1777

→ British advance

□ Fort

< 15 >

would gain the British control of all of New York and isolate the New England colonies from the others. The Americans would then be too weak and divided to continue the Revolution, Burgoyne hoped.

The British lieutenant general would lead the main attack himself, invading New York from Canada, and moving south through Lake Champlain and the Hudson River Valley to Albany. At the same time, a second force in Canada would move down the St. Lawrence River and through Lake Ontario to Fort Oswego, under the command of Colonel Barry St. Leger. From there, this second force would march east to Albany. A third force would be part of Howe's army moving up the Hudson from New York City to join with the other two British forces at Albany. This three-pronged attack was meant to give the British control of the Hudson-Champlain waterway all the way from New York City to Canada.

In June 1777, Burgoyne arrived in Canada to set the plan in motion. The British made little effort to keep their plan secret, so the Americans knew what Burgoyne was up to from the beginning. A physician who supported the patriot cause, Dr. James Thacher, noted in his diary:

> The three [British] armies are to form a junction at Albany. Here, probably, the three commanders are to congratulate each other on their mighty achievement and the flattering prospect of ending the rebellion.... A very active campaign is to be expected, and events of the greatest magnitude are undoubtedly to be unfolded.[4]

Thacher's prediction was remarkably accurate. But even he could not have foreseen how great the magnitude of the events would be. The stage was now set for the battle of Saratoga, the war's turning point.

PART TWO

SARATOGA:
THE TURNING POINT OF THE AMERICAN REVOLUTION

In early July 1777, as Americans celebrated the first anniversary of the Declaration of Independence, General Burgoyne's army struck. With very little opposition, the British captured Fort Ticonderoga, a sturdy stone fort on the southern end of Lake Champlain.

Fort Ticonderoga was expected to be a major obstacle to the British invasion. The 2,500 defenders of the fort, however, felt overwhelmed by the size of the force advancing against them. When the British moved cannons to a hilltop overlooking the fort, the American commander decided to abandon Ticonderoga. Under cover of darkness on July 5, the Americans retreated south.

A Great Victory for the British

Burgoyne's invasion force had sailed down Lake Champlain in a fleet of 9 ships and 180 Canadian boats, called "batteaux." The British commander led an army of 9,000 men, including 4,200 British regulars, 4,000 German mercenaries, 400 Indian warriors, and several hundred American loyalists and Canadians. Burgoyne's fleet was jammed with food, cannons, ammunition, supplies, and even the families of many of his officers.

The British viewed the capture of Ticonderoga as a great victory. Several weeks later, when the news reached London, King George III is said to have rushed into the queen's chambers shouting, "I have beat them! Beat all the Americans!"[1]

Far to the south in Pennsylvania, Washington was stunned by the news that the fort had fallen. He had counted on General Philip Schuyler, the commander in the North, to see to it that "Fort Ti" was properly defended. But Schuyler was in Albany trying to enlist additional troops when the fort fell. Congress voted to remove Schuyler from command and sent General Horatio Gates to replace him.

< 17 >

< 18 >

The Americans who abandoned Fort Ticonderoga made their way to Fort Edward, a crumbling fortification on the east bank of the Hudson River. It was located about midway between Fort Ticonderoga, to the north, and Albany, to the south. There the Americans were joined by Schuyler, who had rushed north with all the soldiers he could muster. The Americans now had about 4,500 men, but that was not enough to hold the dilapidated fort. Once again, they abandoned their position and began a series of retreats south toward Albany.

By mid-July, events seemed to be unfolding just as Burgoyne had planned. The Americans appeared to be retreating in a disorganized way. The second force of Burgoyne's three-pronged attack would soon be moving in from the west, and Howe would send a third force north from New York.

Storms on Burgoyne's Left and Right

From mid-July on, Burgoyne's carefully woven plan began to unravel. His troops found that moving south from Fort Ticonderoga was a slow, torturous process. The batteaux had to be hauled overland from Lake Champlain to Lake George by soldiers who slogged through dense, mosquito-infested forests in mid-summer heat. As the Americans under Schuyler retreated, they had chopped down towering pines to block the primitive forest paths. They had also rolled boulders into creeks, creating dams that turned the roadways into swamps. The British did not take control of Ford Edward until July 30. It had taken them three weeks to advance less than 50 miles.

Since his supplies were running low, Burgoyne decided to send an expedition into Vermont to seize patriot supplies said to be stored at Bennington. An expedition of 900 men was led by German Colonel Friedrich Baum.

Twenty-three-year-old Jane McCrea was the daughter of a minister at Fort Edward. Her father was a loyalist, and she was engaged to loyalist David Jones, who was a lieutenant in Burgoyne's army.

When the Americans abandoned Fort Edward in July, McCrea stayed behind, hoping to meet her fiancé. Lieutenant Jones offered a reward to two Wyandot braves if they would bring her to the British camp.

On July 27, the two warriors returned to the camp. The soldiers stared in horror. One of the braves carried a scalp that many immediately recognized as the long blond hair of Jane McCrea.

Details of how and why the young woman was murdered were never revealed. Burgoyne was afraid to take any action for fear of losing his Indian allies. One of the British soldiers said later that the two braves had apparently argued over who would collect the reward. As they argued, one of them "inhumanly struck his tomahawk into her skull."[2]

News of the atrocity spread throughout the country. The tragedy may have convinced some Americans that Burgoyne either could not control his Indian allies or else encouraged them to kill Americans. The incident probably led some undecided Americans to join the militia in support of the Revolution, and cost the British loyalist supporters.

The Battle of Bennington

Burgoyne did not know that an energetic American militia commander, General John Stark, had raised a strong force of 2,000 men from New Hampshire and Vermont. On August 16, 1777, Stark's militia attacked Baum's force on a hill near Bennington. One of the Hessian officers gave this account of the battle of Bennington:

> [The Americans] *rushed up the hill...in spite of the heavy volley which we poured in to check them, and finding our* [cannons] *silent,*

The British lost 900 soldiers in the battle of Bennington, while the Americans lost only 70.

they sprang over the parapet [raised earth or stone] *and dashed within our works....*

For a few seconds, the scene which ensued defies all powers of language to describe.... Outnumbered, broken, our people wavered and fell back,...till they were either cut down at their posts...or compelled to surrender.[3]

The victory was a critical one for the Americans and a bitter loss for the British. The Americans suffered only about 70 casualties. Baum and 200 of his men were killed, though, and nearly 700 were taken prisoner. Instead of gaining supplies, Burgoyne lost 900 men—10 percent of his army. The New England militia, Burgoyne

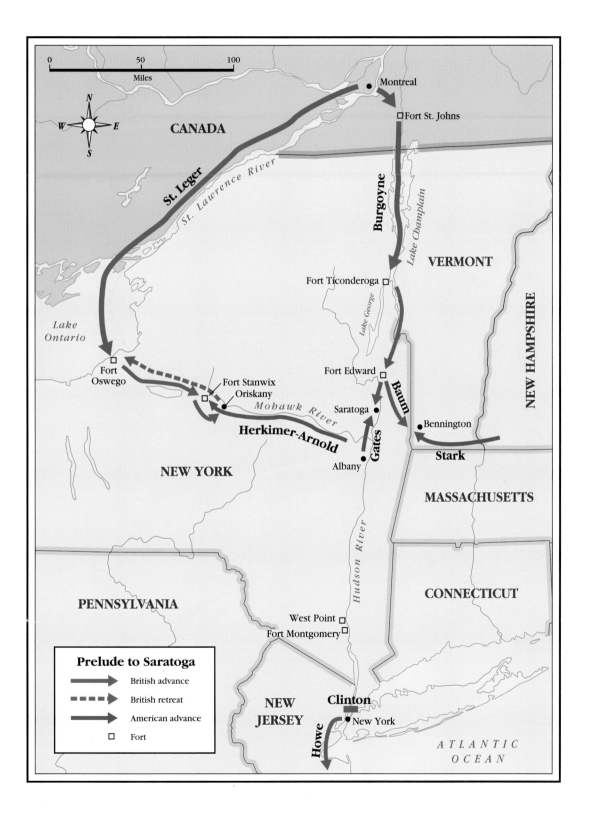

Prelude to Saratoga

→ British advance

⇢ British retreat

→ American advance

□ Fort

< 22 >

wrote, was "the most active and rebellious race on the continent, and hangs constantly like a gathering storm on my left."[4]

The Americans Win Fort Stanwix

Around the same time, another storm was breaking on Burgoyne's right. Late in July, British Colonel Barry St. Leger had sailed down the St. Lawrence River, and through Lake Ontario to Fort Oswego, New York, where his force of 400 soldiers was joined by 1,000 Iroquois warriors.

The British colonel marched east to Fort Stanwix, a rugged, star-shaped fort guarding the approach to the Mohawk River Valley. The fort was defended by 750 Americans under Colonel Peter

General Burgoyne, standing in front of the British soldiers, addresses a group of Indians.

< 23 >

Gansevoort. St. Leger's Iroquois allies quickly surrounded the fort, but Gansevoort's men put up a strong defense. The Americans also managed to sneak messengers out who went to get help.

A few miles to the east, the American militia's General Nicholas Herkimer started for Fort Stanwix with 800 men. At a place called Oriskany Creek, Herkimer's men ran into an ambush planned by St. Leger. Although Herkimer and most of the officers were hit, the militia men fought furiously, and the Iroquois fighting with St. Leger suffered heavy casualties. Gansevoort's force continued to hold out at Fort Stanwix and waited for reinforcements. One hundred miles to the east, Schuyler, who remained in command until Gates arrived on August 19, sent 950 men under General Benedict Arnold to relieve the Americans at the fort. The Iroquois were convinced by a messenger of Arnold's that thousands of Americans were on the way. In a panic, they abandoned St. Leger. Left with only his 400 men, St. Leger decided to withdraw from Fort Stanwix and return to Canada. The second prong of Burgoyne's plan was suddenly gone.

The Eve of Saratoga

Still at Fort Edward, Burgoyne found his position rapidly deteriorating. British supplies were now so low that he was forced to reduce rations by one third. Many of his Indian allies had vanished, and dozens of Germans had deserted.

To make matters worse, Burgoyne received a disturbing letter from Howe stating that he would not follow the original plan by marching north from New York City. Howe had other ideas. "My intention is for Philadelphia," Howe wrote, "where I expect to meet Washington [and the main Continental Army]."[5] Howe apparently thought that Burgoyne and St. Leger could easily take command of the Hudson River Valley without his help. He did mention, though,

General John Burgoyne, known as Gentleman Johnny, was one of the favorites of King George III. Burgoyne was a member of Parliament and a playwright, as well as a soldier. He was often ridiculed for writing pompous proclamations to his troops and to the enemy, copies of which he sent to Parliament.

John Burgoyne

loved the general. He delivered his orders with precision and coolness."[6]

Burgoyne also had his critics, however. They said he moved his troops too slowly and was more concerned with his own comfort than with meeting the enemy.

Born in London, he married the daughter of the 11th Earl of Derby, and moved to France for several years. Upon his return to England Burgoyne rejoined the army. He proved to be a courageous leader in the Saratoga campaign. British Sergeant Roger Lamb wrote of him: "General Burgoyne shunned no danger. His presence and conduct animated the troops, for they greatly

Some months after the surrender, Burgoyne was allowed to return to Great Britain, where he faced considerable criticism in Parliament and the newspapers for the disaster at Saratoga.

The criticism died away after the final British defeat at Yorktown, and he was made commander-in-chief in Ireland. Burgoyne, however, retreated more and more into private life, focusing on his career as a dramatist. He was moderately successful at this, but would always be

that he would leave a force in New York City under General Henry Clinton, who would do whatever was needed.

Burgoyne could only hope that the urgent message he now sent to Clinton would bring the help he desperately needed. To the

remembered best for his defeat in the battle of Saratoga.

Lieutenant Colonel Barry St. Leger was a member of a noble Scottish family, and he was known as a cocky, tough-minded soldier. During the battle for Fort Stanwix, St. Leger warned the defenders that if they did not surrender, he would unleash his soldiers and Iroquois warriors on the homes and farms of the entire Mohawk Valley. He was furious when the desertion of the Iroquois forced him to abandon his mission, but he felt he had no choice but to retreat.

William Howe, like most of the British officers, was a member of an aristocratic family. He had established a reputation for leadership and bravery during Britain's war with France. In February 1775, as a major general, he was sent to America, arriving in time to take part in the battle of Bunker Hill. A year later, he was made commander-in-chief of all British forces in America.

Even though Howe had taken Philadelphia and had defeated Washington's army at the battle of Brandywine, he felt that the government was not giving him enough support. These feelings led him to submit his resignation in early 1778. His brother, Richard, was commander of the British fleet in America and he, too, resigned because he felt inadequately supported. Parliament conducted a formal inquiry into their behavior, but the matter was soon dropped.

Both men eventually rejoined the military and went on to further promotions. William was made a full general in 1793. He resigned 10 years later because of a long, painful illness which finally claimed his life in 1814, at the age of 45.

British Secretary of State for the colonies, Lord George Germain, Burgoyne wrote, "I little foresaw that I was to be left to pursue my way through such a tract of country, and hosts of foes, without any cooperation from New York.... I yet do not despair."[7]

< 26 >

Early in September, the British placed batteaux side by side, in effect making a bridge of boats, and crossed the narrow upper Hudson River at Saratoga (present-day Schuylerville). They moved south cautiously and established camp only four miles from the Americans.

Gates Takes Control

While Burgoyne was wondering how to force his way through to Albany, General Horatio Gates arrived there and took control of all American forces in that region (both Continental Army and militia units), replacing Schuyler. Gates immediately moved the army north, toward the British, to a place called Bemis Heights. It was near the hamlet of Stillwater, only about 10 miles from Saratoga. There, a brilliant volunteer from Poland named Thaddeus Kosciuszko, a colonel of engineers, planned a defensive network. Kosciuszko established a series of log fortifications, with cannons overlooking River Road, 100 feet below. The hilly land was cut by ravines and was heavily wooded. There were a few acres of cleared farmland that included an abandoned settlement called Freeman's Farm.

By mid-September Gates had nearly 9,000 men, mostly Continentals. More militiamen were arriving every day, inspired by the great victory at Bennington. Washington, preparing to defend Philadelphia against Howe's army, managed to send about 600 men from the Continental Army and 350 Virginia riflemen. The riflemen, led by Colonel Daniel Morgan, were known as "Morgan's Rifles." Arnold, who had helped the American forces to defend Fort Stanwix, headed for Saratoga as well.

The battle of Saratoga was about to begin. Although it is referred to as "the battle," it was actually two battles, separated by a lull of two weeks. Most of the fighting took place around Bemis Heights, especially on Freeman's Farm.

Thaddeus Kosciuszko was one of several European volunteers who performed heroically in America's struggle for independence. Born of Polish parents in what is now Lithuania, Kosciuszko studied military engineering at war colleges in Warsaw and Paris. He volunteered his services to the Continental Congress in 1776 and was given the rank of colonel of engineers. British as well as American military leaders were greatly impressed by the strong fortifications he prepared for the battle of Saratoga.

Thaddeus Kosciuszko

After Burgoyne's surrender, Kosciuszko spent two years planning and overseeing construction of the fort at West Point. Late in the war, his engineering talent and skill as a military planner helped the Americans in several battles in the South. After the war, he received the thanks of Congress and was promoted to brigadier general.

Kosciuszko returned to Europe where he spent ten years leading the fight for Polish independence against Russia and Prussia. Although the revolution failed, he emerged as one of the greatest heroes in Polish history. In 1797, Kosciuszko returned to the United States. Congress presented him with $18,000 in pay that was owed him, made him an American citizen, and granted him 500 acres of land in Ohio. After his death in 1817, the provisions of his will were carried out: His Ohio land was sold, and the proceeds were used to help free slaves. Much of the money was used to establish one of the nation's first schools for African Americans, in Newark, New Jersey.

The First Battle of Saratoga

At 10:00 A.M. on September 19, 1777, a cannon shot was fired—the signal for the British to begin their advance. Burgoyne had divided his army into three columns, commanding the center column himself.

John Stark

John Stark was a tough-minded New Hampshire farmer who fought with British forces against France during the Seven Years' War. When the American Revolution began, he raised a militia regiment that performed heroically at the battle of Bunker Hill. He joined Washington's Continental Army and again performed well at the battles of Trenton and Princeton. Stark was so furious at being passed over for promotion, however, that in March 1777, he resigned and went home.

Burgoyne's invasion led Stark to return to action. He again raised a militia. This time, however, he insisted that his force of 1,500 men operate independently of the Continental Army. His strategy and leadership led to the brilliant American victory at Bennington. Congress finally recognized his achievements by making him a general in October 1777, and he served under Washington for the rest of the war. Refusing any further public service, Stark retired to his farm, where he died in 1822 at the age of 93.

Nicholas Herkimer was a successful merchant in the Mohawk Valley, where he built an elegant brick house. As a brigadier general of the New York militia, he organized an 800-man force to relieve the troops at Fort

An injured Herkimer continued to direct his forces at Oriskany.

Stanwix. They were ambushed at Oriskany, about six miles from the fort. Herkimer's horse was struck and crashed to the ground, shattering the brigadier general's leg.

After he was injured, Old Honikol, as he was affectionately known, had himself propped against a tree and continued to direct the militia. Eventually, Herkimer was carried to his home, where an inexperienced French doctor amputated the shattered leg but could not stop the bleeding. Herkimer died a few days later.

Benedict Arnold was a prosperous young merchant in Connecticut when the American Revolution began. In April 1775, he helped capture Fort Ticonderoga. He then led American troops on an incredible journey of hardship and courage in a failed attempt to conquer Canada.

When Congress promoted five officers who were junior to Arnold to the rank of major general, he was furious. Nevertheless, he rushed to the relief of Fort Stanwix in August 1777 and, a month later, displayed courage and skill on the battlefield at Saratoga. In 1778 he was placed in command of the defense of Philadelphia. There he married his second wife, Peggy Shippen (his first wife, Peggy Mansfield Arnold, with whom he had three sons, had died in 1776) and also made his first contacts with the British. Convinced that his country had treated him badly, Arnold turned traitor in September 1780. He became a brigadier general in the British army and led terrifying raids against his former countrymen in Virginia and Connecticut.

After the war, Arnold went to Great Britain. He and his wife had four more children, three sons and a daughter. He died in 1801, deeply in debt. Although he contributed so much to the American cause, he is remembered only as a traitor.

Benedict Arnold

Horatio Gates

On Burgoyne's left, General Friedrich von Riedesel led the Germans. They proceeded along River Road, which ran parallel to the Hudson River. General Simon Fraser led the column on Burgoyne's right.

The British advanced cautiously over rugged hills and through dense woods, unable to see the Americans positioned on Bemis Heights. Gates was content to wait behind the strong American fortifications. Arnold urged him to move forward, pointing out how dangerous it would be to let the British place artillery on the hills above them. Gates finally agreed to let one of Arnold's regiments, including Morgan's Rifles, advance and find the enemy.

Morgan's Rifles Encounter the Redcoats

A little after noon, as Morgan's riflemen worked their way through the woods on Freeman's Farm into a clearing, they ran into the British advance unit, or "picket." Morgan's Rifles, who were also known as Shirtmen because of the fringed hunting shirts they wore, opened fire with deadly accuracy. The British reeled back, with the Americans in close pursuit.

Suddenly, Morgan's Rifles ran into Burgoyne's main force, and it was their turn to scramble back into the protection of the woods. Morgan frantically tried to regroup his men, signaling them by blowing a "turkey call," something like a whistle used by hunters to

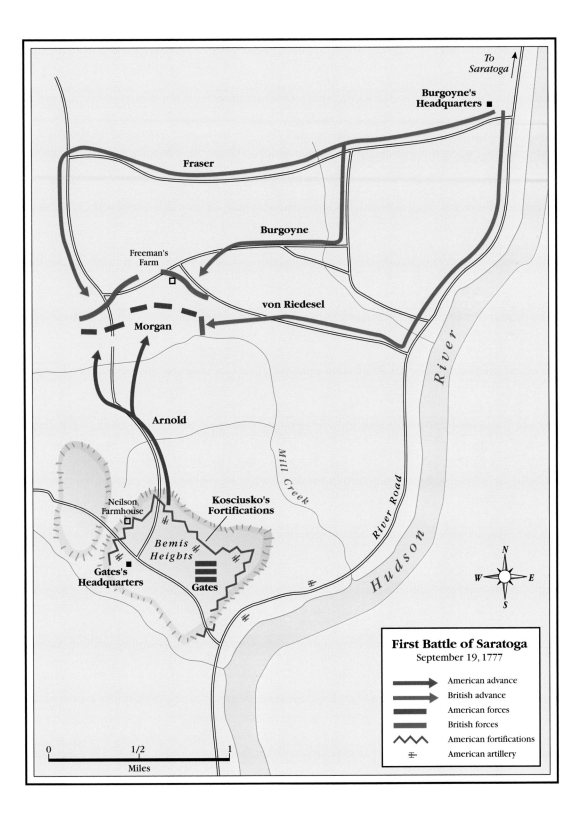

To
Saratoga

Burgoyne's
Headquarters ■

Fraser

Burgoyne

Freeman's
Farm

von Riedesel

Morgan

Arnold

Mill Creek

River

River Road

Neilson
Farmhouse

Kosciusko's
Fortifications

Bemis
Heights

Gates

Gates's
Headquarters

Hudson

N
W   E
S

0   1/2   1

Miles

First Battle of Saratoga
September 19, 1777

→ American advance
→ British advance
▬ American forces
▬ British forces
ⅥⅥⅥ American fortifications
╪ American artillery

< 32 >

attract wild turkeys. At the same time, Gates ordered Arnold to send the rest of his men forward.

The Battle Seesaws

The fighting now became general, and for the next three hours, the two sides surged back and forth across the Freeman's Farm clearing. Time after time, the Americans charged across the clearing, but they were very quickly turned back by showers of grapeshot (clusters of small iron pellets) from the British artillery or by the enemy's bayonets. Each time the Americans fell back, they held their ground on the southern edge of the clearing, while musket fire and Morgan's Rifles blasted at the advancing British.

British Sergeant Roger Lamb described the scene:

A constant blaze of fire was kept up, and both armies seemed to be determined on death or victory.... Men, and particularly officers, dropped every moment on each side. Several of the Americans placed themselves in high trees, and as often as they could distinguish a British officer's uniform, took him off by deliberately aiming at his person.[8]

Baroness von Riedesel, huddled in a nearby house with her three daughters, recalled, "I...shivered at every shot, for I could hear everything. I saw a great number of wounded; and...they brought three of them into the house."[9]

The battle seesawed back and forth across the 350-yard-wide clearing. Neither side was able to take control for long. Late in the day, an American charge, apparently led by Arnold, nearly broke through the British lines. Although some later disputed Arnold's role, one eyewitness said that "Arnold rushed into the thickest of the fight with his usual recklessness, and at times acted like a madman."

< 33 >

Captain Ebenezer Wakefield reported, "Nothing could exceed the bravery of Arnold on this day. He seemed the very genius of war."[10]

Just as the Americans seemed about to drive the British into a frantic retreat, they suddenly heard shouts and gunfire on their right. It was the Hessians, led by von Riedesel, charging up the hills from River Road. They arrived just in time to save the British from disaster, and their lines held.

The British Claim Victory

As darkness closed in, the Americans shouldered their muskets and returned to their camp. From their point of view, the battle was a draw. Major James Wilkinson, an aide to Gates reported: "It was truly a gallant conflict...and certainly a drawn battle, as night alone terminated it, the British army keeping its ground in the rear of the field, and our corps, when they could no longer distinguish objects, retiring to their camp. Yet General Burgoyne claimed a victory."[11]

Burgoyne seemed confident that he had won, even though the British suffered 556 casualties—twice as many as the Americans. In a letter to the commander he had left at Ticonderoga, Burgoyne crowed: "We have had a smart and very honorable action, and are now encamped in the front of the field, which must demonstrate our victory beyond the power of even an American newswriter to explain away."[12]

Interlude: September 20–October 6, 1977

The morning after the battle, a dense fog blanketed the woods and hills. Burgoyne decided he would have to wait a day before renewing his attack on the American position. He actually waited for 17 days. Burgoyne delayed because of some news he received.

Baron Friedrich von Riedesel was regarded as the most able of the German officers who fought on the British side. He arrived in Canada in 1776, bringing with him 2,300 mercenaries. He was in command of the German portion of Burgoyne's army during the Saratoga campaign.

Von Riedesel's wife, Frederike, and their three daughters joined him for the long, difficult march south from

Baron Friedrich von Riedesel

Canada. During the fighting at Fort Ticonderoga and at Freeman's Farm, von Riedesel did all he could to keep his family safe, but he also performed brilliantly in the field.

After the British surrendered, von Riedesel was held prisoner until 1780. One reason von Riedesel was imprisoned for so long may have been his refusal to promise that he would not fight against the Americans again. Upon his release, he continued to serve the British until the end of the war. The von Riedesels returned safely to Europe in 1783.

Simon Fraser was a member of a noble family in Scotland. He served the British cause with dedication and bravery, and Burgoyne relied more on him than on any other officer. Fraser's men also had the greatest confidence in him, partly because he did not hesitate to put himself in danger leading his men into battle.

During the second battle of Saratoga, Fraser was wounded by Morgan's riflemen. He died the next day and was buried that evening. The Americans, seeing a group of

British, opened fire with their cannons. Gates later apologized, saying he had not known that the gathering was a funeral.

Henry Clinton was raised in the American colony of New York, where his father, Admiral George Clinton, served as governor in the 1740s. Henry fought in Britain's war with France, rising to the rank of major general. He was elected to Parliament in 1772.

Clinton returned to service at the start of the American Revolution. He served as second in command of British forces to General Howe and proved his leadership in the battles for New York City in 1776. Howe placed him in command of New York City while he set off to seize Philadelphia. Always a cautious man, Clinton was reluctant to send aid to Burgoyne during the Saratoga campaign, apparently worried that doing so would endanger New York City. That failure to act doomed Burgoyne's army.

When Howe resigned from his position as commander-in-chief in 1778, Clinton replaced him. His most

Simon Fraser

successful campaign was the capture of Charleston, South Carolina, in 1780, which handed the Americans their worst defeat of the war. After the final British defeat at Yorktown, Virginia, Clinton returned to Great Britain and wrote his account of the war. In 1790, he re-entered Parliament. Clinton was made Governor of Gibraltar in 1794, but died a year later while serving in that office.

< 36 >

On Sunday, September 21, the British commander finally heard from Clinton in New York City. Clinton told him he was planning to attack Fort Montgomery, on the lower Hudson, and then advance toward Burgoyne. This was welcome news, and Burgoyne decided he would wait for Clinton and his men. They might already be approaching. Burgoyne sent a messenger with a note urging speed. If he and Clinton could attack the Americans from both north and south, they would be victorious. During the wait, Burgoyne had his men build a series of wooden barricades, called "redoubts," stretching from the river up the hills through Freeman's Farm.

Day after day, the two armies remained where they were, facing one another. The British, operating in enemy territory, saw their rations fall to near-starvation levels. Burgoyne wrote:

Baroness Frederike von Riedesel

The armies were so near that not a night passed without firing and sometimes concerted attacks on our advanced pickets. No foraging party could be made without great detachments to cover it.... I do not believe either officer or soldier slept during that interval without his clothes.[13]

The lull in the fighting gave Baroness von Riedesel a chance to enjoy the autumn foliage, and to make a keen observation:

< 37 >

The country was magnificent, but all the people had gone to strengthen the American army.... Every inhabitant is a born soldier and a good marksman; in addition, the thought of fighting for...freedom made them braver than ever.[14]

Militia units continued to arrive at the American camp every day. By the end of September, the army had expanded from 9,000 men to more than 13,000. Although Gates clearly had the advantage, he waited for the British to make a move before he attacked. He said of Burgoyne, "Perhaps his despair may dictate to him to risk all upon one throw of the dice; he is an old Gamester and in his time has seen many chances."[15]

No News from Clinton

By early October, Burgoyne was truly desperate. He still had no news of Clinton's approach. What the British commander did not know was that the messenger carrying his frantic note to Clinton had not gotten through. The message had been placed in a small silver ball, which was customary. When the messenger was caught, he swallowed the ball, just as he was supposed to. His captors saw him swallow something, a Connecticut soldier recalled, and "the general ordered the regimental surgeon to administer a strong emetic, which in its powerful operation occasioned him throwing up a silver ball the size of a bullet, which on being cleansed and opened was found to contain the note."[16]

Clinton, unaware of Burgoyne's desperate situation, did not attack Fort Montgomery until October 6. Ten days later, he sent only 1,700 men up the Hudson to help Burgoyne, while returning to New York City with most of his force.

In Burgoyne's camp, Fraser and von Riedesel advised a retreat to Fort Ticonderoga. Instead, Burgoyne decided on a limited attack,

< 38 >

hoping to establish an artillery position on the hills above the Americans that would make it difficult for them to hold their ground.

The Second Battle of Saratoga

On the morning of October 7, Burgoyne renewed his attack. He led a force of 1,500 of his most experienced troops.

Shortly after noon, Gates was told that the enemy was approaching. "Well, then," the American commander said, "Order on Morgan to begin the game."[17]

Morgan's riflemen immediately set out. In the past, Morgan and his men had been part of Arnold's command. But perhaps as a result of a bitter dispute between Arnold and Gates before the battle, Arnold was dismissed as the action began. Furious at how he was treated, Arnold was forced to remain in camp.

Morgan's Rifles Rush "Like a Torrent"

After waiting for Morgan to get into position, Gates ordered an advance against the center of the British line. "True to his purpose," Major Wilkinson wrote, "Morgan at this critical moment poured down like a torrent from the hill and attacked the right of the enemy in front and flank [side]. [Major Henry Dearborn, under Morgan's command]...pressed forward with ardor and delivered a close fire, then leapt a fence, shouted, charged and gallantly forced [the British] to retire in good order."[18]

As the Americans advanced, Wilkinson reported that "in the square space of twelve or fifteen yards lay eighteen [British soldiers] in the agonies of death, and three officers propped up against the stumps of trees, two of them mortally wounded, bleeding and almost speechless."[19]

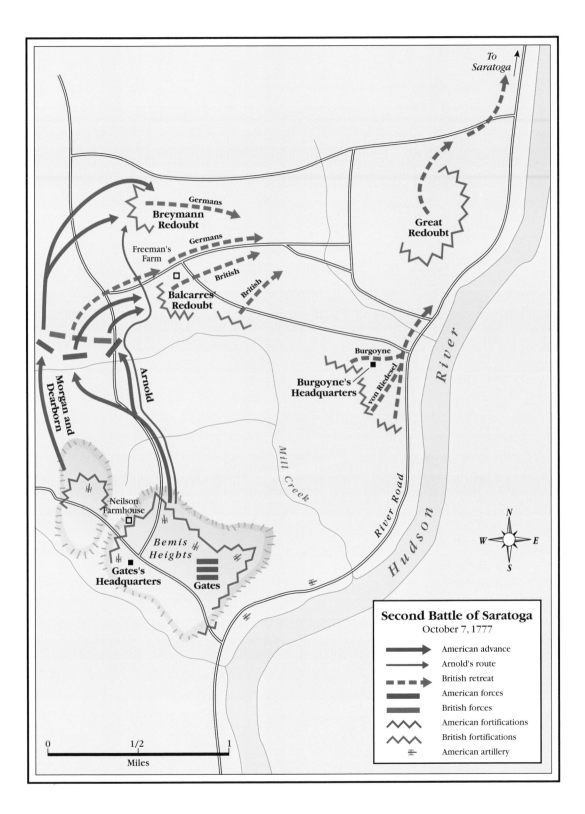

Germans

Breymann Redoubt

Freeman's Farm

Germans

British

Balcarres Redoubt

British

Great Redoubt

Burgoyne

Burgoyne's Headquarters

von Riedesel

River

Arnold

Morgan and Dearborn

Mill Creek

River Road

Neilson Farmhouse

Bemis Heights

Gates's Headquarters

Gates

Hudson

To Saratoga

N
W   E
S

| 0 | 1/2 | 1 |

Miles

Second Battle of Saratoga
October 7, 1777

American advance
Arnold's route
British retreat
American forces
British forces
American fortifications
British fortifications
American artillery

Horatio Gates was born in Great Britain and served in the British Army before moving to Virginia in 1772. He served on Washington's staff before being appointed to command the Northern Department of the Continental Army. In his reports on the Saratoga fighting, he made no mention of Benedict Arnold because of the running feud between them. Largely on the basis of his own reports, and those of his aide, Major James Wilkinson, Gates was hailed as "the hero of Saratoga." (Some members of Congress who disliked Washington started a movement to have Gates replace him as commander-in-chief. Fortunately for the American cause, that effort failed.) In 1780, without consulting Washington, Congress placed Gates in charge of the Southern Department of the Continental Army. He suffered a disastrous defeat at the battle of Camden (North Carolina) and fled from the battlefield. Gates was immediately replaced, but later his friends in Congress officially cleared him of blame.

After the war, Gates returned to his plantation in Virginia. His wife died in 1784, and Gates remarried in 1786, at which point he freed his slaves and moved to New York City. He served a term in the New York Assembly (1800–1801), then lived quietly in retirement until his death in 1806 at the age of 78.

Daniel Morgan was one of the Americans' most skilled battlefield leaders—and also one of the most unusual. As a young man, he fought with the militia in support of Britain during the Seven Years' War. But following an argument, a British officer had him flogged with 500 lashes. He never forgot his treatment at the hands of the British and often used the story to inspire his men in their fight for freedom.

In June 1775, Morgan joined the Continental Army and organized a company of 500 Virginia riflemen—Morgan's Rifles. He and his men joined Benedict Arnold in a disastrous attempt to invade Canada late

At this point, Arnold, on horseback and in defiance of Gates, appeared through the clouds of gunsmoke and rode furiously into the thick of the fighting. As one American soldier recalled, "He

in 1775. After Morgan's brilliant success at Saratoga, he spent the winter with Washington's army at Valley Forge. In 1779, Morgan resigned and returned to his Virginia farm, claiming his painful arthritis had forced him to retire. His real reason for leaving may have been the failure of Congress to promote him.

After the American defeat at Camden in 1780, Morgan rejoined the Continental Army, and Congress finally made him a brigadier general. His greatest military success was at the battle of Cowpens in January 1781, when he defeated a powerful British and loyalist regiment. That victory seriously weakened the British and contributed to their decision to retreat to Yorktown, Virginia, where the war's final battle took place. After Cowpens, Morgan once again retired to his farm.

In 1794, George Washington, now the first president of the United States, called Morgan out of retirement to help suppress a rebellion

Daniel Morgan

over taxes in Pennsylvania. Morgan led troops into Pennsylvania and the rebellion, which became known as the Whiskey Rebellion, melted away without a fight. Morgan was elected to Congress in 1797 and served one term in the House of Representatives, finally retiring for good in 1799.

behaved...more like a madman than a cool and discreet officer."[20] The men cheered when they saw Arnold and pressed forward, forcing the enemy back.

< 42 >

Burgoyne, seeing that his lines were being overwhelmed, ordered his men to retreat behind the redoubts, or fortifications, that ringed the British camp. For a moment, Fraser rallied his men to stay where they were, but then he was hit by one of Morgan's crack shots, and his troops fled to the redoubts.

Arnold now led an attack on Balcarres' Redoubt. It was the strongest British fortification, a wall of logs 8 feet high and nearly 500 yards long held by a force under Major the Earl of Balcarres. The British and Germans, firing muskets and cannons at point-blank, or very close, range forced the Americans back.

Arnold's "Mad Prank"

Then Arnold spotted another American regiment advancing toward the enemy on his left. In a daring move that Wilkinson described as "a mad prank,"[21] Arnold spurred his horse, dashed across the battlefield between the opposing forces, and joined the new attack.

As cannons and muskets roared, Arnold led the assault on the Breymann Redoubt, held by German soldiers under Colonel Heinrich von Breymann. (Von Riedesel and his men were closer to the river during this attack.) With his men close behind him, Arnold led the way through an opening in the redoubt. His horse was shot from under him, and Arnold went down with a bullet in his leg. But even as he fell, he was shouting words of encouragement: "Rush on, my brave men! Rush on!"[22]

The British and Germans, Wilkinson wrote, "retreated in disorder, leaving their gallant commander [Breymann] dead on the field. By dislodging this corps [unit], the whole British encampment was laid open to us."[23] As darkness fell, however, the Americans were too exhausted to go further. Burgoyne led the remnants of his assault force behind what was called the Great Redoubt, a long fortification protecting the British camp.

During the assault on Breymann Redoubt, Benedict Arnold urged his men on, even after being wounded.

The battle was over, and this time there was no doubt about who had won. Out of the 1,500 men Burgoyne sent into the battle, 600 had been killed or wounded, while the Americans suffered only about 150 casualties. Burgoyne's once proud British army was now less than 6,000 men, and they were pinned against the Hudson River by an American force that outnumbered them by more than two to one.

Retreat and Surrender

The British and German officers clung to the hope of retreating to Fort Ticonderoga and trying to hold out there until Clinton could come to their aid. But even as they moved slowly north in the days following the battle, the Americans pressed in on them, hampering

< 44 >

every movement with steady cannon and rifle fire. Farther north, the militia under John Stark captured the squad Burgoyne had left at Fort Edward. At the same time, 1,300 Massachusetts militia took control of the hills on the eastern side of the Hudson, opposite the town of Saratoga.

By the time the British reached Saratoga on October 10, they could go no further. Baroness von Riedesel described the last days:

> *We were finally obliged to take refuge in a cellar.... On the follow-*
> *ing morning, the cannonade again began.... Eleven cannon balls*
> *went through the house, and we could plainly hear them rolling over*
> *our heads. One poor soldier, whose leg they were about to ampu-*
> *tate, having been laid on a table for this purpose, had the other leg*
> *taken off* [by the cannon ball]...*in the very middle of the opera-*
> *tion.... In this horrible situation we remained six days.*[24]

On October 13, Burgoyne finally asked for a cease-fire, and the two sides negotiated the terms of surrender. Gates was generous: The prisoners would be marched to Boston and allowed to return to Great Britain after promising not to take up arms against the Americans again. He agreed to Burgoyne's request to call the sur-render a "convention," which the British commander hoped would make it sound like less of a disaster. Gates made the surrender terms generous so he could end negotiations quickly—he was afraid Clinton might be approaching from the south. Neither he nor Burgoyne could have known that Clinton's modest expedition would turn back to New York City, except for the 1,700 men who would be sent from Fort Montgomery to make contact with Burgoyne.

On Friday, October 17, 1777, the British and Germans marched out of their camp, laid down their weapons, and emptied their ammu-nition boxes. Then they marched past the victorious Americans.

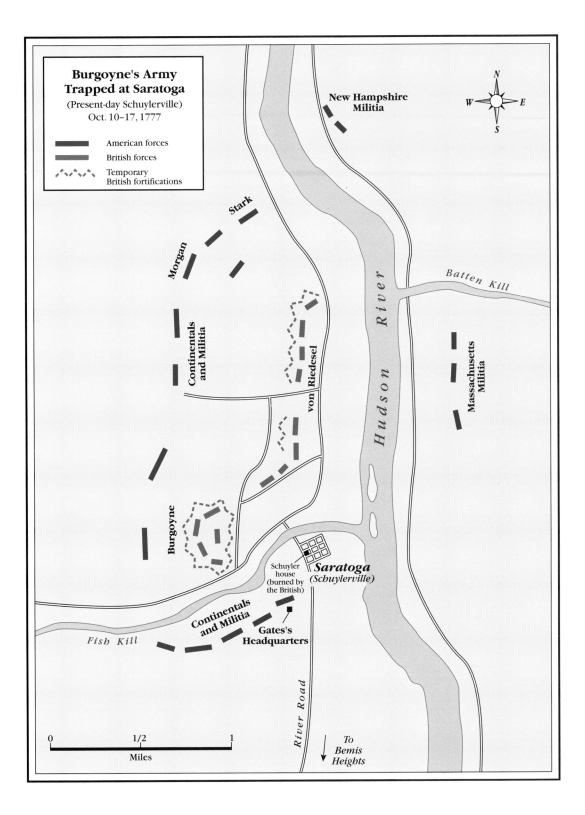

**Burgoyne's Army
Trapped at Saratoga**

(Present-day Schuylerville)
Oct. 10–17, 1777

American forces
British forces
Temporary
British fortifications

New Hampshire
Militia

N
W   E
S

Stark

Morgan

Continentals
and Militia

Batten Kill

Hudson River

von Riedesel

Massachusetts
Militia

Burgoyne

Schuyler
house
(burned by
the British)

Saratoga
(Schuylerville)

Continentals
and Militia

Fish Kill

Gates's
Headquarters

River Road

0   1/2   1
Miles

To
Bemis
Heights

Burgoyne, mounted on a horse (on the right), prepares to surrender.

A British officer recalled, "I shall never forget the appearance of their troops on our marching past them; a dead silence universally reigned through their numerous columns...I must say their decent behaviour during the time (to us so greatly fallen) merited the utmost... praise."[25]

Gates, in a plain blue coat, faced Burgoyne in his brilliant scarlet uniform. Burgoyne handed him his sword in surrender, and Gates courteously returned it. Burgoyne's great plan for ending the war with a quick British victory ended instead with his surrender of 7 generals, 300 other officers, and 5,500 soldiers. The two battles, which took place mostly around Bemis Heights, are called the battle of Saratoga because that is where Burgoyne formally surrendered.

The Outcome: Turning Point of the Revolution

The battle of Saratoga was a stunning victory for the Americans and a devastating defeat for the British. The very size of the triumph was astounding—never before had so large a British force surrendered to an enemy. More important, it breathed new hope into the American cause and dramatically changed the course of the war.

< 47 >

For Americans, news of Burgoyne's surrender could not have come at a better time. While the troops under Horatio Gates were battling Burgoyne's army in the North, Washington had been unable to protect Philadelphia from Howe's force in Pennsylvania. Washington's outnumbered Continental Army had fought well, but lost major battles at Brandywine Creek and Germantown. The Continental Congress was forced to flee to Lancaster, the British triumphantly entered Philadelphia, and Washington's ragged army retreated to Valley Forge, where they would suffer through a winter of cold and hunger. If the British had won at Saratoga as well, the American cause might have collapsed.

New Confidence and a New Ally

The victory at Saratoga gave Americans a new confidence in the ability of their troops to defeat the well-trained and experienced British redcoats. The British, too, gained a new respect for the discipline and battlefield skills of the Americans. They had thought that the patriot militiamen would flee the battlefield rather than stand up to a British army. Instead, the Americans at Saratoga had carried the fight to the finish, claiming one of the most important victories in the Revolutionary War. One of the officers who surrendered at Saratoga summed up what the British had learned: "The courage and obstinacy with which the Americans fought were the astonishment of everyone, and we now became fully convinced they are not the contemptible enemy we had hitherto imagined them, incapable of standing a regular engagement."[26]

The most important long-range outcome of Saratoga was its influence on France. For two years, American diplomats, led by Benjamin Franklin, had been urging the French government to aid the American cause. The French had been quietly supplying ammunition, but they were not willing to risk another war with Great

Benjamin Franklin helped persuade the French government to recognize American independence. Here he is pictured with Louis XVI, King of France.

Britain, especially since the patriots seemed to have little chance of winning. The patriots' dramatic victory at Saratoga persuaded the French that the Americans could win. Within a few weeks, Franklin began negotiating a treaty. France recognized American independence and joined the war against Great Britain. The British

< 49 >

now had another enemy to fight, and the Americans could count on receiving desperately needed money, weapons, and supplies from their new ally.

The battle of Saratoga and the Americans' resulting alliance with France did not hasten the end of the war, however. The conflict continued for four more years and, during that time, the Americans often had reason to despair. But Saratoga showed them what they could achieve, and it successfully blocked the British strategy of isolating the New England colonies from the others. The British leaders were so shocked by Burgoyne's surrender that they sent a peace commission to meet with the Continental Congress. But the peace offer came too late. Congress would not discuss peace unless American independence was recognized, and so the commissioners returned to London without accomplishing anything.

The British Change Their Strategy

The British then shifted their war strategy. Early in 1778, Howe was replaced by Clinton, Philadelphia was abandoned, and Clinton concentrated his forces around New York City. From New York, he launched a series of invasions of colonies in the South, hoping to find more loyalist support there.

From 1778 to 1781, most battles were fought in the South, where patriot militia repeatedly prevented the British from gaining control. The end came in the autumn of 1781 at the siege of Yorktown in Virginia. While French warships kept the powerful British fleet out of the area, Washington's American and French troops forced the British to surrender, after a siege that lasted for eight days. Although the peace treaty ending the American Revolution was not signed until 1783, no major battles were fought after Yorktown. The Americans had overcome all odds and won their independence.

HISTORY REMEMBERED

America's battlefield parks are more than monuments to the dramatic struggles involved in creating and preserving our nation. They also offer an opportunity to walk in the footsteps of those who fought in these historic battles—the common soldiers as well as the great battlefield leaders like George Washington, Daniel Morgan, Horatio Gates, and a host of others.

Visiting battlefields gives us a sense of what it was like to take part in critical moments of American history. We can see the same stone walls, forests, clearings, rivers, and buildings that men fought and died to control.

From time to time, these battlefield sites are endangered by the needs of our modern urbanized society. Several sites have been threatened by developers' plans for highways and shopping malls. Saratoga National Historical Park was closed for a time in 1995 when government belt-tightening cut off funds for staffing the park.

In the past few years, however, a growing number of Americans have become involved in preserving these important parts of our heritage.

Saratoga National Historical Park

When visitors stand on the open field at Bemis Heights, they look down on a scene that vividly reflects the landscape of those fateful days in the autumn of 1777. Here and there, a cannon faces the narrow ribbon of the Hudson River below. Dense woods still cover the hillsides and the jagged ravines. Farm fields and a scattering of houses interrupt the forest growth.

One can picture Burgoyne's redcoats struggling through thickets and trees to the clearing of Freeman's Farm, while von Riedesel's blue-clad Germans advance along River Road. On the near side of the clearing, one can imagine Morgan's Rifles, in their hunting shirts, opening fire from behind rail fences and trees.

< 51 >

A "patriot" loads a cannon at Saratoga National Historical Park.

A tour road winds through Freeman's Farm and Bemis Heights for nine miles. The road is open from April 1 to November 30, weather permitting, but hikers use much of the road throughout the year. There are ten main stops along the road, enabling visitors to see exactly where key fortifications were located. One of the stops is outside the Neilson farmhouse, which was used by at least one American general as his headquarters. The house has been restored to its 1777 appearance, and volunteers in period dress give living history demonstrations on the grounds throughout the summer. The last stop on the road is the burial site of British General Simon Fraser.

Location and Address Saratoga National Historical Park is located near the village of Stillwater, New York, about 40 miles north of Albany. (Note: Don't confuse the town of Saratoga Springs with the battle of Saratoga; Saratoga Springs was founded later. The historic town of Saratoga, where Burgoyne surrendered, is

< 53 >

located at present-day Schuylerville, about eight miles north of the battlefield.)

Saratoga National Historical Park, R.D. 2, P.O. Box 33, Stillwater, NY 12170. Telephone: (518) 664-9821.

Operating Hours The Visitor Center is open from 9:00 A.M.–5:00 P.M. daily except Thanksgiving, Christmas, and New Year's Day.

Entrance Fees $4.00 per car. Hikers and bikers, $2.00 per person age 17 and older; 16 and under, free.

Exhibits and Events The Visitor Center contains excellent interactive audio-visual displays, as well as exhibits of weapons and equipment. There is also a well-stocked bookstore. A 20-minute film, called *Checkmate on the Hudson*, and the well-informed staff both offer a wealth of fascinating information. Guided hikes are also provided by park personnel over the extensive roads and trails. Schedules for these hikes, and a map of the route, are available at the bookstore. Daily demonstrations at the park include cooking, music, dancing, crafts, and storytelling from the eighteenth century. There are also military demonstrations of camp life, weapons drills, and cannon firing. Additional information is available from The Friends of Saratoga Battlefield, 648 Route 32, Stillwater, NY 12170. Telephone: (518) 664–9821.

Related Points of Interest

Schuyler House

Eight miles north of the battlefield, the Schuyler House is located on the Hudson River in Schuylerville. The British burned the original house and mill in September 1777, shortly before the first battle of Saratoga, but the house was rebuilt a few months later. The house is open for tours during the summer and is also the setting for living

< 54 >

history demonstrations, ranging from eighteenth-century crafts, music, and costumes, to weapons displays. Information about these events is available at the Saratoga National Historical Park Visitor Center. Just over a mile west of the Schuyler House is the Saratoga Monument, a 155-foot-high tower built in 1883 to commemorate Burgoyne's surrender. A winding stairway leads to an observation platform with a dramatic view of the battlefield to the south. The monument will be undergoing restoration until sometime in 1999.

Location and Address The Schuyler House is on Broad Street in Schuylerville, New York.

Operating Hours Friday–Sunday and holidays, 9:30 A.M.–4:00 P.M., June 20–September 1.

Entrance Fees Admission to the house and monument is free.

Exhibits and Events Guided tours of the house and grounds are conducted by volunteers in period costume throughout the hours of operation. For more information about events, contact the Visitor Center at Saratoga National Historical Park.

For an even richer exploration of Burgoyne's entire three-pronged campaign, visitors can tour related battlefield sites.

Fort Stanwix

After years of neglect, Fort Stanwix was completely reconstructed in the 1970s. Located in downtown Rome, New York, the full-scale reproduction contains most of the buildings as they looked in 1777, including the barracks, a drawbridge, and a "bomb proof" (an underground shelter that could withstand a direct hit by a cannon ball).

Location and Address 112 East Park Street, Rome, NY 13440, near Exit 33 off the New York State Thruway (I-90). Telephone: (315) 336-2090.

A woman dressed in period costume spins wool at Fort Stanwix.

Operating Hours Daily, 9:00 A.M.– 5:00 P.M., April 1–December 31.
Entrance Fees $4.00 per person; children under 10 free.
Exhibit and Events A film called *The Siege of Fort Stanwix* is shown at the Visitor Center, located in the West Barracks. In the museum building, behind the Visitor Center, there is an interesting display of weapons and artifacts unearthed by archaeologists during the restoration of the fort. Park personnel offer guided tours of the fort and will provide special assistance for handicapped visitors. Between Memorial Day and Labor Day, volunteers give living history demonstrations, which include weapons firing, cooking, crafts, and military drills on the Parade Ground. Dates and times for special events are available at the Visitor Center.

Fort Ticonderoga National Historic Landmark

Perhaps no fort in North America has been the scene of more battles—or changed hands more times—than Ticonderoga. The strategic location of the fort, at the junction of Lake Champlain and Lake George, made it the key defense of the Hudson River corridor between Canada and New York City. Originally built by the French

< 56 >

in 1755, the fort changed hands during France's long war with Great Britain. The British controlled it until 1775, when it was seized by an American force led by Benedict Arnold and Ethan Allen. The British occupied it briefly during the Saratoga campaign, and destroyed it when they realized they could not hold it. The impressive star-shaped fort and outlying fortifications are fully restored.

Location and Address State Route 73, Ticonderoga, NY 12883. Telephone: (518) 585-2821.

Operating Hours The fort is open daily from early May to late October. Hours are 9:00 A.M.–6:00 P.M. After Labor Day, the fort closes at 5:00 P.M.

A fife and drum corps plays a march at Fort Ticonderoga.

< 57 >

Entrance Fees Adults $8.00; children 7–12 $6.00; children under 7 are free.

Exhibits and Events One reason for the rather high entrance fee is that Fort Ticonderoga has one of the most ambitious events programs of any historic landmark or battlefield park. Daily events, for example, include march music by a fife and drum corps, plus several cannon firings. Among the special events held each summer is an encampment in early September, at which more than 500 volunteers, in uniform, demonstrate weapons and tactics used in the various battles associated with the fort. For exact dates and times of this and other events, contact the Visitor Center.

Bennington Battle Monument

Southeast of Ticonderoga, in Vermont, is the Bennington Battle Monument—a 306-foot-tall obelisk, a slim stone structure that tapers to a point. It offers a panoramic view of the site of John Stark's militia victory over Burgoyne's expedition.

Location and Address North of Bennington Center at 15 Monument Circle, Old Bennington, Vermont, 05201. Telephone: (802) 447-0550.

Operating Hours Daily, 9:00 A.M.–5:00 P.M., from mid-April to October 31.

Entrance Fees $1.50 per person ages 13 and up; $ .75 for ages 6–12; children 5 and under admitted free of charge.

Exhibits and Events A model of the battle of Bennington is on display, with miniature officers and soldiers in position. Special events include musket demonstrations, a Fourth of July celebration, and on August 16, a reenactment of the battle of Bennington.

CHRONOLOGY OF THE REVOLUTIONARY WAR

September 1774	First Continental Congress meets in Philadelphia.
April 1775	British army and the Massachusetts militia fight at Lexington and Concord near Boston.
May 1775	Massachusetts and Vermont militias capture Fort Ticonderoga on Lake Champlain in New York.
June 1775	Second Continental Congress appoints Washington commander of the Continental Army.
June 1775	Americans fight at the battle of Bunker Hill.
August 1775–July 1776	American attempts to invade Canada fail.
March 1776	British evacuate Boston for New York.
July 1776	Continental Congress declares the United States independent from Great Britain.
August–November 1776	British under General Howe drive Washington's army out of New York.
December 1776	Washington defeats the British at Trenton, New Jersey.
January 1777	Washington defeats the British at Princeton, New Jersey.
June–October 1777	British General Burgoyne's invasion of New York fails.
July 7, 1777	British capture Fort Ticonderoga.
July 30, 1777	British capture Fort Edward.
August 6, 1777	General Herkimer is defeated at Oriskany.
August 16, 1777	General Stark is victorious in the battle of Bennington.
August 24, 1777	General Arnold relieves Fort Stanwix.
September–October 1777	Howe defeats Washington at Brandywine and Germantown, Pennsylvania, and occupies Philadelphia.

< 59 >

September 19, 1777	The first battle of Saratoga
October 7, 1777	The second battle of Saratoga
October 17, 1777	British General Burgoyne surrenders at Saratoga.
Winter 1777–78	Continental Army at Valley Forge
February 1778	France and the United States form an alliance.
June 1778	British leave Philadelphia for New York; Washington battles them at Monmouth Courthouse, New Jersey.
July 1778	General Clark captures British posts in the Northwest.
December 1779	British capture Savannah, Georgia.
February–May 1780	British besiege and capture Charleston, South Carolina.
July 1780	4,000 French troops under Rochambeau arrive at Newport, Rhode Island.
September 1780	American General Benedict Arnold commits treason and joins the British.
January–May 1781	Mutinies occur in the Continental Army.
May–August 1781	Cornwallis spars with Lafayette in Virginia and fortifies Yorktown.
August 1781	Washington and Rochambeau march south to join Lafayette and trap Cornwallis at Yorktown.
September–October 1781	Siege of Yorktown
October 1781	Cornwallis surrenders Yorktown.
April 1782	Peace talks begin in Paris between Britain and the United States.
September 1783	Treaty of Paris signed, ending the American Revolution.

FURTHER READING

Athearn, Robert G. *American Heritage History of the United States,* vol. 3, *The Revolution.* New York: American Heritage Co., 1988.

Cuneo, John R. *The Battles of Saratoga: The Turning of the Tide.* New York: Macmillan Co., 1967.

Fritz, Jean. *Traitor: The Case of Benedict Arnold.* New York: Penguin Books, 1989.

Gay, Kathlyn and Martin Gay. *Revolutionary War* (Voices from the Past Series). New York: Twenty-First Century Books, 1995.

Hakim, Joy. *From Colonies to Country* (History of the United States Series). New York: Oxford University Press, 1993.

Longguth, A.J. *Patriots: The Men Who Started the American Revolution.* New York: Touchstone, 1990.

Meltzer, Milton, ed. *The American Revolutionaries: A History in Their Own Words.* New York: Thomas Y. Crowell, 1987.

Murphy, Jim. *A Young Patriot: The American Revolution As Experienced by One Boy.* Boston: Houghton Mifflin Company, 1996.

The Revolutionary War Soldier at Saratoga (Soldier Series). Minneapolis, MN: Capstone Press, 1991.

Steins, Richard. *A Nation Is Born: Rebellion and Independence in America* (First Person America Series). New York: Twenty-First Century Books, 1993.

WEB SITES

A good way to explore the dozens of World Wide Web sites dealing with the American Revolution is to go to the Revolutionary War home page. Here you will find an extensive listing of sites on subjects ranging from John and Abigail Adams to Yorktown, the final battle of the war. The Web address is:

http://www.multied.com/Revolt

Another Web site is even more comprehensive, with listings of Revolutionary War era music, art, newspapers, and daily life, as well as events in the war itself. This site, called "The American Revolution On Line," is located at:

http://users.southeast.net/~dixe/amrev/index.htm

For a listing of articles and sources focusing on the battle of Saratoga, see:

http://www.spa.net/battle/battle.htm

National Park Service personnel at Saratoga National Historical Park are currently developing a Web site dealing with such topics as living history demonstrations and archaeological research at the park.

Take a trip to other historical parks and landmarks at:

http://www.nps.gov/frsp/files/npssite.htm

From the index, you can go to sites describing the major features at each park or landmark, how to get there, what activities are held, dates and hours of operation, and admission prices.

SOURCE NOTES

Part One

1. Quoted in David C. King et al., *United States History* (Menlo Park, CA: Addison-Wesley Publishing Co., 1986), p. 98.

2. Quoted in Samuel Eliot Morison, *The Oxford History of the American People* (New York: Oxford University Press, 1965), p. 224.

3. Quoted in John Gabriel Hunt, ed., *Words of Our Nation* (New York: Random House, 1993), pp. 22–23.

4. James Thacher, *Military Journal of the American Revolution* (North Stratford, NH: Arno Press, 1969), p. 189.

Part Two

1. Bard McDowell, *The Revolutionary War: America's Fight for Freedom* (Washington, D.C.: National Geographic Society, 1967), pp. 111–112.

2. Quoted in George F. Scheer and Hugh F. Rankin, *Rebels and Redcoats: The American Revolution Through The Eyes of Those Who Fought and Lived It* (New York: The World Publishing Co., 1957), p. 260.

3. Ibid., p. 264.

4. Ibid., p. 266.

5. Quoted in McDowell, *The Revolutionary War*, p. 114.

6. Richard Wheeler, *Voices of 1776: The Story of the American Revolution in the Words of Those Who Were There* (New York: Penguin Books, 1972), p. 222.

7. Quoted in John R. Cuneo, *The Battles of Saratoga: The Turning of the Tide* (New York: The Macmillan Company, 1967), p. 38.

8. Quoted in Wheeler, *Voices of 1776*, p. 222.

9. Quoted in William L. Stone, trans. and ed., *Letters and Journals Relating to the War of the American Revolution* (North Stratford, NH: Arno Press, 1968), p. 117.

10. Both quotations in Samuel Eliot Morison, *The Oxford History of the American People* (New York: Oxford University Press, 1965), p. 248.

< 63 >

11. Quoted in Wheeler, *Voices of 1776*, p. 224.

12. Quoted in Scheer and Rankin, *Rebels and Redcoats*, p. 276.

13. Ibid., pp. 227–278.

14. Quoted in Stone, *Letters and Journals*, p. 144.

15. Quoted in Morison, *The Oxford History*, p. 248.

16. Quoted in Scheer and Rankin, *Rebels and Redcoats*, p. 278.

17. Quoted in Joseph E. Stevens, *America's National Battlefield Parks* (Norman, OK: University of Oklahoma Press, 1990), p. 32.

18. Quoted in Wheeler, *Voices of 1776*, p. 237.

19. Quoted in Cuneo, *The Battles of Saratoga*, p. 66.

20. Quoted in Scheer and Rankin, *Rebels and Redcoats*, p. 281.

21. Ibid.

22. Quoted in Morison, *The Oxford History*, p. 248.

23. Quoted in Wheeler, *Voices of 1776*, p. 239.

24. Quoted in Stone, *Letters and Journals*, p. 170.

25. Quoted in Cuneo, *The Battles of Saratoga*, p. 87.

26. Quoted in Rebecca Gruver, *An American History* (Menlo Park, CA: Addison-Wesley Publishing Co., 1978), p. 87.

OTHER SOURCES

Melzer, Milton, ed. *The American Revolutionaries: A History in Their Own Words*. New York: Thomas Y. Crowell, 1987.

Morris, Richard B. and editors of *Life*. *Life History of the U.S.*, vol. 2, *The Making of a Nation*. New York: Time, Inc., 1963.

Purcell, L. Edward, and David F. Burg, editors. *The World Almanac of the American Revolution*. Mahwah, NJ: World Almanac, 1992.

Schlesinger, Jr., Arthur M. *The Almanac of American History*. Greenwich, CT: Brompton Books, 1993.

INDEX